TO Sabrina

FROM The Parr Family

DATE June 2010

You've Only Just Begun

First edition for the United States, its territories and possessions, and Canada published in 2009 by Barron's Educational Series, Inc.

Copyright © Gillian & Darryl Torckler, 2009
Original title of the book: Graduation
Copyright © David Bateman Ltd.

All inquiries should be addressed to:
Barron's Educational Series, Inc.
250 Wireless Boulevard
Hauppauge, New York 11788
www.barronseduc.com

ISBN-13: 978-0-7641-6184-1
ISBN-10: 0-7641-6184-9

Library of Congress Control Number: 2008932018

First published in 2009 by
David Bateman Ltd.
30 Tarndale Grove
Albany
Auckland, New Zealand

Book design by Alice Bell

Printed in China through Colorcraft Ltd.,Hong Kong

9 8 7 6 5 4 3 2

You've Only Just Begun

INSPIRATION FOR THE GRADUATE

Gillian and Darryl Torckler

BARRON'S

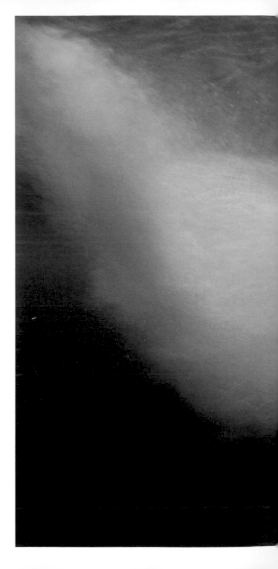

A teacher affects eternity; he can never tell where his influence stops.

Henry B. Adams

Celebrate your achievement
Celebrate your stamina
Celebrate your teachers
Celebrate your family

Celebrate you!

Hide not your talents.
... What is a sun-dial in the shade?

Benjamin Franklin

Visualize your journey

think of what you want

It takes as much energy
to wish as it does to plan.

Eleanor Roosevelt

imagine how to get there

Do not go where the path may
lead; go instead where there is no
path and leave a trail.

Ralph Waldo Emerson

overcome the boundaries

and keep your dreams alive.

Imagination is the
highest kite one can fly.

Lauren Bacall

Patience and passage of time
do more than strength or passion.

Jean de La Fontaine

Set targets

To infinity and beyond!

Buzz Lightyear

stay focused

Some succeed because
they are destined to;
most succeed because
they are determined to.

Anatole France

*take one step
at a time*

Be not afraid
of growing slowly,
be afraid only
of standing still.

Chinese proverb

*on your
chosen path*

don't always pick
the easy route

but keep moving forward.

Grab hold
of opportunities

as they pass by

but remember— some things are not as they seem.

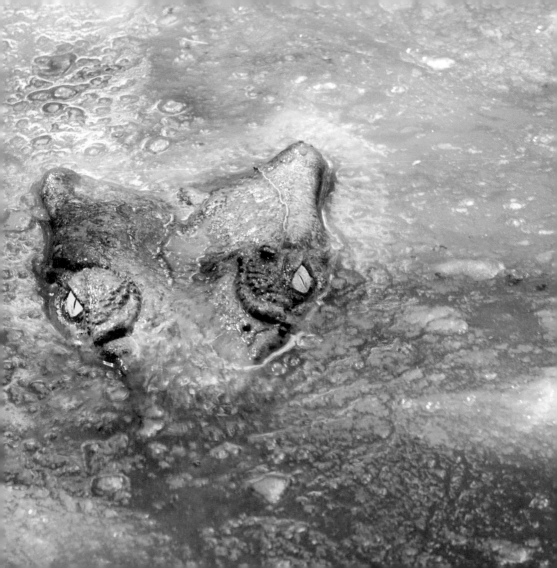

Success is getting
what you want;
happiness is wanting
what you get.

Dale Carnegie

Take risks

when you need to

The shell must break
before the bird can fly.

Alfred, Lord Tennyson

but only when you know the odds.

Behold the turtle. He makes progress
only when he sticks his neck out.

James B. Conant

Realize when you're beat

When just about everything is
coming your way, you're obviously
in the wrong lane.

Anonymous

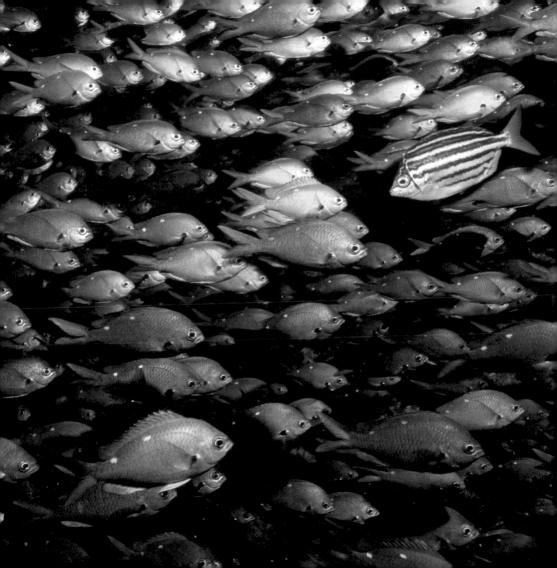

learn from the experience.

Wise man:
One who sees the storm
coming before the
clouds appear.

Edgar Watson Howe

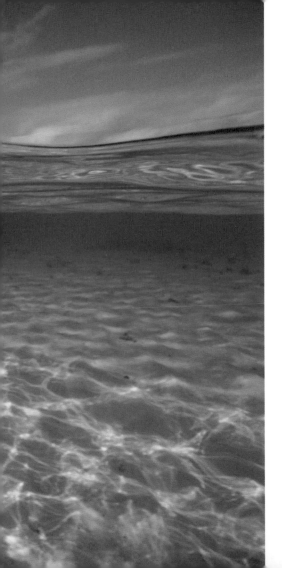

Learn
how to ask
for help.

Start again but remember your mistakes

Failure is simply
the opportunity to
begin again, this time
more intelligently.

Henry Ford

and listen with open ears.

Learn to listen.
Opportunity sometimes
knocks very softly.

H. Jackson Brown, Jr.

Remember your team

combine your individual strengths

*to reach
your common
goals.*

The man who
graduates today and
stops learning tomorrow
is uneducated the
day after.

Newton D. Baker

It isn't over yet.

Man's mind, once
stretched by a new
idea, never regains its
original dimensions.

Oliver Wendell Holmes, Jr.

You've come
a long way

but all you've
learned is
only valuable
if you keep
learning.